# Harlot

whoops!
← the harlot can't
spell

for Alan

from
" a woman
black with
a wasted
face.

23 feb
2004
KGB

**Also by Jill Alexander Essbaum:**

*Heaven* (University Press of New England)

*Oh Forbidden* (Pecan Grove Press)

# Harlot

Jill Alexander Essbaum

No Tell Books 2007
Reston, VA

*For Rahab, Tallulah, Joan of Arc…*

Copyright © 2007 by Jill Alexander Essbaum

Published by No Tell Books, LLC

notellbooks.org

ISBN: 978-0-6151-6131-0

Cover Design: Meghan Punschke

Cover Art: Cynthia Large

Proofreader: Joseph Massey

# Contents

Take a harp, go about the city, thou harlot that hast been forgotten;
Make sweet melody, sing many songs, that thou mayest be remembered.

Isaiah 23:16

In the sweaty, passionate, filthy embrace, in all of its delicious and time-solving power, in the midst of that embrace there is no difference, no separation between the spiritual and the profane.

Leonard Cohen

Every harlot was a virgin once.

William Blake

# And it Came to Pass

That you were naked and I wanted you.
With the awkward undulations of a virgin, I wanted you.

By my concubinal urges and the use I once put
to doubtful hours, when the salt

began to sour, when the salt lost its saltness.
When I was given to wandering the heart's incongruous

chambers as night unraveled
like thread from a spindle,

I wanted you/ And I wanted you like a snake in love, /
*hell-bently*. And I wanted you in the olive grove,

where the harvester gathered slowly but my hand roamed greenly.
And I wanted you in the abbey, kneeling penitently,

a postulant in the Church of the Kiss,
faithful to an audience

of one. And I wanted you from the knocking until
the last goodbye. From our first catastrophe into our final.

I wanted you when I had and when I lacked.
I wanted you when the kingdom cracked

and *All Else* was fallen into. I wanted you when I died
and rose again. When rumors of impending Christs survived

whole afterlives of woebegone redress. And when dry bones
exploded from their graves of sand. And when I winnowed

chaff from grain. And when I thrashed you upon my cornfloor.
And when I bedded you in my manger.

I wanted you
like a wound

aches for the dagger digging
into it, so bloody

and brutal and black.
I wanted you like *that*.

# The Assignation

Tonight, she will dream of him
in sequences. How the sharp, slim

cut of his well-tailored suit
sliced like a knife through a very ripe fruit

the final share of her resolve
into twin, bitter halves.  How tall

he stood against her, pestle-ing
the mortar of her pelvis.

And how the air, tight with disaster,
thinned to a stratospheric

black. She will dream of her maneuvers
and his rocket. How she flipped him like a lever,

how he plugged into her socket,
how he strangled her waist with the corset

of his straitjacket hands. How she surged
with urgencies

so adamant and so Jezebel,
he all but shrieked. How he took out her tortoiseshell

combs with his teeth. How she undid his buttons,
slid down his briefs, and feasted like a glutton

two feet above his knees. How the cloister
of her thighs wept liturgies and hours,

13

but how white and well worth it were the tremors and the woe.
And how his bliss, succinct as snow,

won her over. And she will dream, then, of his eyes, the pair of them.
How they thawed the ice of her arms like paraffin

beneath a lit wick's flame.
And the way

he unloosed with his stare
that knotty nest of hair

below her belly, above her pout.
And how it all *went down*

clumsily, like a sophomore poet's go at anapest.
How he fumbled up the ample of her breast,

but how oh how that only made her ardor
puff and swell. As well, how she quivered

like new brandy in a crystal glass.
And how—*and alas*—

the bright of afternoon
bent too soonly

into shadow, and how the droll, drab blue
of the rented room

relented when the night came on.
And how they put their clothes back on

slowly, lolling over each fasten.
How she'd planned to tell her husband

she'd gone shopping,
stopping

at three distinct boutiques before she found
that one, flesh-toned wraparound

for which she had been pining
*(and how that wasn't outright lying).*

And how against the setting of the TV's busted static,
her husband had said "*That's nice.*" And how he'd meant it.

## Judas Hausfrau

Judas Hausfrau.
The wife of Lot.
I do not let

well-enough alone.
I do not care to.
But you already know

this. Unmapped,
I am the lay
you called *Strange*

*Land*, your risk
and periphery, all borderline.
And yet, I am the exact edge I'm

on. *Verge, lip.*
Hell's Jezebels.
I serve you well.

But the night matron
will make her rounds.
And I will put my hands down

holes they oughtn't
go in. Sweet little
gleaming thing, all spittle

and spunk. *Christ,*
*it is never enough*: Covens
of bedroom men, convening.

A swarm of drones. Mounts
of lancers, hussars, horsemen.
A sea of weeping men

with hard-ons,
hard, hard
upon me. *Pick a card—*

it's always the queen.
Sir, I owe you *nothing.*
My dowries

are collapsed. I'm the ghost
your wedding photo snapped
into clean halves.

A knock-off joypop
good for a tumble or two.
*Mrs. You,*

my white dress shines
as black as the night.
*I do not fight*

*it.* On the eve of scars
and jags, I am chrism
in the mouth.

*Schlaf, Traum.*
I wear ropes around my neck
and watch my back.

I cellar the coins.
I purse the salt.
I am tall

in my sins.
*Don't you forget it.*
This target

is tainted. Square up
and take your aim.
The stained satin. The Satan.

# Poem

After the minute hand husked past seven,
Before it lumbered to thirty-nine.
After the headache, before the aspirin.
After Jesus, but long before Christ.

After the preface, before the epilogue.
After I winnowed the chaff from your grain.
After we kissed, before your hard-on.
After I waxed. Before you waned.

After the Scotch but before the highball shattered.
After you came, before I arrived.
After we fucked, before it mattered.
After *good riddance*. Before *goodbye*.

# The Men We Marry, the Men We Fuck

This one kissed me beneath the stars.
That one fondled me up the stairs.

This one confessed his sins but to God.
That one demanded his pity aloud.

This one drove me to the store.
That one drove me like a car.

This one gave me violets and asters.
That one brought me violence and disaster.

This one wed me in the chapel.
That one ate me like an apple,

And he was as handsome as he was doomed.
Lovely as lust, but fickle as the moon.

This one built a house to live in.
That one fed me glass and poison.

This one tended a kindled hearth.
That one threw me to the dirt

And by the greenbrier patch we tangled,
Hand to thigh and lip to nipple.

The men we marry, the men we fuck:
This one doubly filled my cup,

That one used me up.

# Song of Bird, Dirge of Branch

We stumble over pleasantries.
The fool of my demeanor glistens.
I finger the wineglass absently.
You lower the lights, draw the curtain,
And I want you more than I want to breathe.
A nightjar flits in the hazel tree.
You tempt me atop you. *Easily.*

You bathe my mouth in similes.
My lips are loamy, lush as Eden.
We speak in tongues, so fluently.
I bow my head and you *Amen.*
So I pray you like the rosary.
A waxwing nests in the cherry tree.
For you, I would do *anything.*

I warble desperate melodies,
The harlot's psalm, a martyr's hymn.
I'm naked in my beggary.
As I go down, you rise again
And I nail my flesh to the cross of your need.
A winter wren shivers in the hawthorn tree.
What's there to lose? *Oh, everything.*

You leave as I sleep, inaudibly.
Only the moon knows how it happens.
Too white, she mocks my misery.
The fissure of this heartbreak widens.
How green-gilled of me to presume a reprieve!
A starling falls from the dogwood tree.
And you will be the death of me.

# Young Magdalene's Prayer

She asks for a sign, there is no sign to give her
but that her valleys end in mystery,
and her peaks verge the heights of a restless
derring-do. It is always like this:

The damp hands of sincerity that pet her lily,
dandle her rose, and rarely any answer apropos enough
to matter. Nevermind the flimflam fists
of boys. They loom as thunderpeals, distant

professions of rain to come. *Come*, proclaims the river
that divides her. Windblown, her grassland geographies.
Wild brush, she blushes. Her uncharted land demands.
She asks for a sign, but the sign is a stumbling block:

*Incubate the mustard seed and it will ripen and rub you
raw.* She sees it in a dream: A king, as divine
as her desires are deep, arrives like a night-thief
to ravish her troves. And just what's safe-keeped

in that box of hers? Not even the angels know
whether it's flesh or fire *(though it seems she's got herself
a thorn, and it makes each month for blood).* She asks
for a sign, but the scrolls have sealed against her swelling seas.

Privates are kept private. Unmentionables won't be
mentioned. Even Holy Writ is locked like lips, like the lips
of the mothers on the street where she lives, mothers
who've cable stitched their mouths with jaundiced wool

and knowing glances, their lukewarm arms made weak
beneath long sleeves of personal defeat. *How will the bride
make ready for the feast?* She can hardly imagine
what she might do with her fingers.

## An Oracle Concerning the Melancholic Concubine

Sometimes you feel you've a touch of the broken heart,
when the orchid of evening wilts into nighttime,
when the darkness is not yet deep.

When you are tipsy with the grief of his leaving,
a flutter in your dovecot, when you chatter like a magpie,
staggering. When, unlucky wren, you are all sin

or shining. *Fine, fine*, you pledge aloud, though you are lying.
When you move against what he remembers of you.
When you are two steps ahead, but arrested.

*En passant*, when you are a pawn for his play
or an intention in his imperative mood. When bare verbs
subject you to their brutal futility. When he abuses you

in his absence, when his somnolence blacks you out.
When you relax and when you tense. When at last you give in
and you anchor down, crouched between his wedge and sleeve.

When you cannot help it. When it comes so easily.

# Sadness is a Tower

Queer box, this. The one in which I'm fixed,
rapt between what's gesture and what's gist
of me, as I yarn out the scarf of this story I've knit.

Miles above the twilit city,
the wailing hurrah of its flicker dizzies
me dumb. The window, occasioning to be witty,

warns *Objects Below Are Exactly As Far*
*Away As They Appear. So Don't Jump, Dear.*
And anyway, I don't. Not this year.

Instead, like the prize pupil in the School
of the Ominous Eye, I stand in its center, coolly
framed by the composure of the glass's good

sheen, the sheer of the pane *(what a treatment!).*
Blindly, I raise and lower the vents
of the shade. I count the blades. There's discipline

in despairing, see? I burn a certain effort
anguishing, as high as I am and as expert
(in that, there's condolence, comfort

enough). What a smooth room. Doorless,
I'm in a jam. What a shame. The dolorous
troposphere thins. Resultingly, my tropes

endear not anyone. I'm bricked tight in like a toad
in a cornerstone: Surely croaking, surely alone,
and nothing to do but dirge or die. Below,

a swoon of citizens exist to never
look up. I remember those days. In lovers'
arms and by vapors  hazing up from the river

bank, I too asserted blood oaths of devotion.
I did not lift my eyes. Not *once*. Not *then*.
(They won't either.) Graven,

god-ghastly image, sadness is an icon emphatically
weeping tears of bone. Sadness is static.
It doesn't go. Or, like the tedious orbit

of the hour hand about the white, wide face of the clock,
sadness moves so slowly, it seems to be stopped.
It perches like a bird, crows like a cock,

and the weathervane informs: Here Come Storms.
Sadness is a worm in blunt halves. You're
severed from yourself.  Sadness is the unicorn

that for a horny season came to call, but never returned.
Sadness is something you earn. As did I, so can you. A cavern
of black riches. A wealth of woe to burn.

And, yes, sadness *is* a tower. It is a place the body craves,
that plot apart where the heart won't scar or break.
Oh. *It's too late.*

# Minx

*Proverbs 23:27*

A lewd woman is a very deep ditch.
A wayward wife is a narrow pit.

She is long and curved like a jackknife clam,
helixed and sharp as a wentletrap.

A stopgap measure of carnal enjoyment.
If she sucks you off in private

there are public consequences.
She is intemperate, discretionless

and dire. A fiend on fire,
a demoniac, writhing.

Rarely does she tire of the riling or the thrashing.
And the time she has is always smashing.

And she is *ravishing.* And she will ruin you.
And her brooding tendencies will tend to confuse you,

and her fiend heart hearkens to innumerable perversities.
And she gets her hands *dirty,*

converting any would-have-been saints into heathen.
She boils you in her cauldron, she terrifies your children,

she slaughters your oxen,
she knocks your wooly socks off—

she vexes like the vixen that she is.
She's wild, defiant, with crafty intent.

*Yes*, she will rosin your fiddlestick, Master.
And wiggle on your manhood, if you ask her.

And you'll cradle in her arms entire nights
suffering the thrill of her delights,

and you may well coo at every ruse she tries.
But if she says she loves you, *she lies*.

# The Clockmaker's Mistress Knows Complications †

Lover,
where does the past go
when it's over?

Dumb pendulum.
You do not move. So ours,
indeed, is the wrecking hour.

*Mean time*: Nine's for nothing.
Despise me if you have to.
I did not set my wrist to this.

Ten will either tempt
or torment you.  Even so,
mine is a hipbone that's hardly

indifferent. Sandglass, I rattle
with hard shards. Stop, *watch*:
Eleven chimes. *Oh why, oh wife.*

Once, and under an odd,
August moon, you drew me
into you. It was

a motion towards
endless possibility.
But for a second

infinity, I would wind myself
around your stem. Again
and again and again.

And later will simply be *Too Late*.
Therefore, let this intolerable ache
become my calm

but intricate ennui. Midnight.
I oscillate blindly. I am your warp,
your flawed balance wheel.

Do not ask me how I feel.
And do not let me touch you,
I might mean it. *One a.m.*

I feed on habits of dolor
and solitude. *Two.* I loved you
like the wild plum loves

the teeth sinking into it,
wetly, willing, quiet as quartz.
*No remorse.* And no escape-

ment. Still, I tick
towards your unrung bell.
*It's three.*

I am not doing well.
The heart's alarm appeals
to ill-luminous hands.

But you set me atop your mantel.
And you fob me at the end of a chain.
I am clockwise to your ways:

A locked, blackwood long-case.
Your chronic, ecliptic restraint.
The bezel, bedeviled edge of your face.

# Despair is the Only Unforgivable Sin

*The name of the Slough was Despond.*
John Bunyan, *The Pilgrim's Progress*


O holiest error of a night, this mad,
     malicious night, a supine night, bright

as bile, but anyway, inauspicious.
     Bedraggled night, delicious as doom.

A night over which no angel will swoon.
     *O moon.* O eye of God, unblinking.

And, yes, I have been drinking. Through black,
     vacant hours and all the blank minutes

between them: O night, *fifth gin,*
     and the hot, hard, heavy of a dark,

creeping spleen. O pit-middle of shadow,
     through which the limbic incubus shifts

and reels. O eels. In the sea of my bed,
     they're electric. They wish me dead.

*O my head.* I am awake and cannot
     take it. A spendthrift ache says it hurts

because it has to. *The bastard.* As if
     anyone's last words were ever *truly* true.

O virtue—*Ich habe dich vergessen.*
     What a mess. O midnight and her cheap,

wide eyes, her grim, conniving hassles.
        O Hansel sorts of hunger as were pined-for

by the witch. O last-ditch longing
        of these broke-down bones. O alone.

O how I walk, my back to my own back,
        ill-cyclic and clinically succinct. Hoot owl,

I've been hoodwinked. A deep sleep comes,
        both with and without dreaming.

Anymore would be too much. O fuck.
        O ravage. O poison. O gift. O season

of makeshift betrayals. O am I adverbial:
        *Bleakly, forebodingly, balefully me.*

This is no small-scale anxiety. Into my living death,
        Lord, come. For you have haunted me

enough with your Jesus and your cross, besides.
        And Father, though Almighty,

polices as he pleases. O my wreck,
        the rubbernecked and the naked

stare with an onlooker's gape, crawling
        the lanes of my veins, by their vehicles

and their vices. And I would try it likewise,
        were I able. *O Devil.* I wear

my blasphemies like jewelry. They glint
        when the light hits them, sorely.

I abhor Thee, my oversight. O revelries,
    scarified, throttled or slight.

O shackle. O scruple. O scalpel.
    *O knife.*

# The Villagers Warned Me About You

The Wheelwright spoke, *He'll run you in circles!*
The Lawyer affirmed there was little appeal.
The Watchmaker seconded: *All complication.*
The Meter maid cited: *No validation.*

The Stargazer charted each path of our defeat.
While the Pastor swore, *It's blasphemy!*
The Fishwife angled there were others in the sea.
The Schoolmarm instructed me to mind my seat.

The Cobbler eschewed you, said you were a heel.
The Wet Nurse expressed that you'd milk me dry.
*He'll bleed you in vain,* gushed the local Stigmatic.
The Private Investigator called you a dick.

The Fire Marshall cautioned you would burn down my house.
The Smithy bellowed, and the Drunk demanded proof.
The Postman was frank, said you wouldn't deliver.
The Barber polled his shop regarding keen-edged razors.

The Gambler wagered that you were a long shot.
The Janitor leaked, *There's a hole in his bucket.*
The Barkeep poured over bitters and thirsts.
The Butcher revealed that you were the *worst.*

The Artist sketched out how you would frame me.
In the Realtor's appraisal, you'd likely quitclaim me.
The Orthodox avowed you would truly incense me.
The Sharpshot gauged that you might not miss me.

The Stripper tittered: *He'll bust your bubble!*
The Seamstress snapped: *Oh, not again?!*
The Vintner whined there'd be sour grapes.
The Mortician laid it out: *The consequence is grave—*

And the Town Fool married you anyway.

# Storms

Once, we sifted clouds for miracles and I,
I danced with my skirt pulled up to my thighs.
You fingered the drizzle and mist at my seam,
And nothing untoward blew through the airstream.

And yet, the hurricane came.
So we masked the weakness of our window's pain
With tape. Those intersecting X's and their gummy residues.
It only rained a day and then I lost you.

# Psalm of Shattering

Oh Lord of Hosts and Nazarenes,
Hear my Psalm of Shattering.
How do I come to feel these griefs?
A little lust is a dangerous thing.

Beneath the orchard canopy
As balm of pear swelled in the breeze
I squeezed his pulse between my knees,
And behaved my hands so shamelessly.

Our eyes belied a hot-blood need.
He stroked my body, crease to pleat.
A passerine purled from the fork of a tree
As he passed his mouth all over me.

But the torture of Christ was shared with thieves.
His was the right cross. The left was for me.
I lumbered up that Calvary
As clouds moved into mystery.

I'm fifty kinds of agony.
And so damn drunk I cannot see.
And so damn sad I cannot breathe.
I meant well, if half-heartedly.

So I laze in a bed of catastrophe,
And sleep these dreams that are not dreams.
I'm guilty of nothing but defeat.
His ardor caroused the unrest in me.

But nothing will rouse the rest of me.

# Crux

I was invited to your torture and I went.
I brought no guest, I bore no gift.

*This will do*, something cold and hard
and small inside me roared.

Weak in your unkind season,
I did not listen.

Atop that hill, upon your cross,
I could not help but awe at all my losses.

Every one, they trilled in the air
like a birdsong dirge. I stared

at you with threadbare eyes
and became kinds of woe I'll never classify

as the sun slid over a sky so blue it shuddered.
I swore I'd not recover.

Oh Man of Sorrow, black as pitch and sleek,
my scapegoat king disguised as sleep,

Dark Creature, grief have ye turned into gall
and we drank of it, *royally*.

And the name of our star was Wormwood.
And I crawled into your casket as a worm would;

my ends were bitter and thrashing.
But lovers are like wings

and one alone will never make you soar.
So mine is a whore's

forehead. I do not blush
with shame. I tell you this

to impress you with my honesty.
These days, I drowse in spindles, loosely,

and upon unspecified linens.
This is no consolation,

as laughter's but an *ess* away from slaughter.
I can and cannot help it, though I ought to.

Christ, if this be dreaming let me
never dream again. A devil's duty,

I ghost through your darkness
better than some, though worse

than most. I suppose
that it pleases you to know

I've atoned for these transgressions.
Therefore: I sign my confession

*Jill.*
*Beneath whom only is Hell.*

# Lament

*Timor Mortis Conturbat Me*

When twilight tires of its terrors.
When the errant anguish of the night thrush erupts
Like a fat, black moon upon an ashfield of urns.
When God, in his bitter infinity prepares a worm to seize me.
When the invincible enemy sees me.
When I burn the notice that confirmed our break-up.
When you notice that I crack-up, but how it's never from laughter.
When sun-up is the zero hour, but I do not merit an ounce of sleep—
The fear of death confounds me.

When I carve, from the bones in my wrist, a flute.
When I prove it to you. When I throb and when I clench.
When you trawl my water with fisherman's fingers.
When I sit quite still and clip your clothes into pieces,
Even as my shattered tearwells swell with stars.
When the door is open but the curtains are drawn,
And the curtains are gauze, and the walls have eyes.
And when the screaming light of Christ casts doubt on me—
The fear of death confounds me.

When I'm pissed on want for lack of wine.
When you coax down my panties with a vulpine tongue.
When perishing atop you, I do not rise up.
When the deed is done and the evidence is hidden.
And when I fall ill with a semblance of sepsis,
And you fill in our ellipses with question marks.
When your damn, dotted heart scars me speechless.
When your arctic stare ice-bounds me—
The fear of death confounds me.

When the end is near and I draw close to Jehovah.
When it is over. When we were lovers.
When Marian apparitions devour the clouds.
*Jesus.* You are handsome.
So I let you put your hand in. And then you demand it.
And it *hurts, hurts, hurts* because it has to, *it has to.*
When you, my disaster, have driven me to drink.
When empties and bottleshards fill the sink.
When a bloodstain slurs through my nightgown's seam—

The fear of death yet confounds me.

But you go on without me.

# Harlot

*(a definition)*

A woman in black with a wasted face,
    Small, bleak girl in a blue satin dress,
        A nervy girl with a rabid pulse,

A loose-of-life lady, a beggar in skirts,
    A kitten at your keys, the witch who wouldn't burn,
        The red spot on Jupiter that could swallow the Earth,

A cavern into which you climb,
    The gangplank bridging swoon and sigh,
        That wee bit of lust you drag alongside,

Who you cast like a pearl before a pig,
    Who you clothe as a housemaid in your wife's rags,
        Who frotts your thigh and bums your fags,

Who cooks the supper and who works the avenue,
    Who has a different name each time she knows you,
        Who swears that she would kill for you,

The early bird that eats the worm,
    An orphan of the universe,
        The coed seducing her teacher mid-term,

She's miracle, spectacle, pinnacle, side-show,
    Manacle, clavicle, tabernacle, afterglow,
        A little button made of bone,

Who lodges in the heart's hotel,
    Who people demand of what they will,
        Who'll do you in the swimming pool

And play Cockney nurse to your Scottish physician,
    A cock-smitten gin-Molly with a sottish disposition,
        The groupie who's made it with all the musicians,

A wily mistress, Zion's daughter,
    That stupor in the gaze of mourners,
        Grave-digger, stone-cutter, hearse-driver, shroud-mender,

Who lies beneath you like a whore,
    And puts good use to sullen hours,
        And blinks back tears of raving terror,

Your whole life's happiness, grey as ash,
    Your piece-on-the-side, your secret stash,
        A hot sauce and a tasty dish,

Who will dance until God falls out of His sky.
    And allow you to handle the merchandise,
        But will engine your Titanic to an iceberg demise,

And will screw you to the wall with scant ado,
    Darkness done, she casts no shadow,
        *Fuck all*, she'll say, *I'm having issues,*

She's the fiction invented for your arousal,
    The serpent you take up and the poison you suckle,
        A frivolous income at your disposal,

And her weary nights wear on worriedly,
    And she fears she may die from lack of sleep,
        And her wide-alive eyes are Eau-de-Nil green,

And her Free States masquerade as Confederate,
    And her tastes run noble, but her talents, proletariat,
        Who flirts with trouble and trouble returns it,

She's your *Sanctum Sanctorum* and your *Hocus Pocus*,
    Whole cities spring up from the ruin she once was,
        She is insane, and she is in sadness,

Who will stick to you as a burr to cloth,
    Who blends her Stoli with Seconal,
        The she-wolf with your crotch in her jaw,

Intransitive verb without an object,
    And if you loved her you should have said it,
        And if you said it, you ought to have meant it,

Rahab, Tallulah, Joan of Arc,
    Hooker, Strumpet, Strap-on, Tart,
        She'll go up like a goddamn spark

And singe your linens and char your plaster,
    And traumatize your mother and appall your pastor,
        And she will do *whatever* you ask her,

The gangly book-mouse who cowers a bit,
    That soft-bottomed Ma with a child on her tit,
        A concubine damp from her sash to her slit—

*Yeah.* That's about it.

# The Heart

Four simple chambers.
A thousand complicated doors.

One of them is yours.

# Why Hast Thou?

Waking, I do not wake.
Here is the fact of it.
My arms ail, unaided.
Your cold is calculated.

Damsel at the door of Father's house,
my Israel bears No Pity.
Evil hour, a Pentateuch of woe,
five stones you throw

at my shadow, simpering.
And yet, beneath the shyberry tree
your red thorn pricks immodestly.
Naked, I know thee,

*fully.* It is a true blue terror,
absolute and emptier than the dress
I have undressed from. I swig
your vinegar, maul the vulgar

throbbing I will come
to underrate. A note on your scissors
reads: *Haunted. Do not use.*
But I do.

I amputate them all.
The laurels, the palms.
The wines I drank, the Christs
of bronze and iron I enticed.

I am the axemaid. I hack and I hew.
The wound—I assume—
will be worse than the scar.
*By far.*

But bleeding, I bleed freely.
It is early, a moist Friday morning.
You leave, so cavalier and quick.
I nearly die of it.

# The Ellipses We Consist Of

Tonight, the eve of any and all regrets,
and still, I am not close enough to pet
your cheek with my beleaguered palms,
these feathering veins, my mottled swans.

The presence of your absence swells the bowl of my hips.
Thirst wrings sobs from my pillow's silk sadness.
So I keen to the rue and dole of knowing
that my bones are far too at home in your going.

A prayer to hush this groan of solitude, my breath
too full of sigh and of shamble. I'd offer you my breasts,
but I'm not able. And then,
for every grief I candle and spin,

you quietly suckle her twin.

## La Linguiste

Singularly, her mood predicated
a comparative level of woe:
Desperate, *desperater*. It was said,

actively, that she was more than tense.
Her face was tight and dark
as a blackletter font. Archaic.

Unreadable. It was as if a conjunction
of bad planets *or/but*-ed her own
passive body. She lived alone,

an independent clause, all vowel
and voiceless. As such, hers was an alphabet
without inflection. She spoke plainly

to the trees and to the house eaves.
And to the door that wasn't there—
*You are a negative construction,*

she would regret aloud, and often.
This went on for years of nighttimes.
She, sleeping, her jaw tight with declension,

a prepositional ache slicing the blade
of her tongue: *Under. Against. On top of.*
*From behind...* But daylight

with its pronounced broad rays would
hiss through the margins of the window shade
and another damn morning would subject her

to an imperfect future. It was a battle of *shalls*
and *wills*. And while it's quite impossible to move
in a straight line when one is in a labyrinth,

even sadists sing love songs to their ligatures
now and again. How it finally happened
to happen is cliché enough for freshman comp:

A colleague from the college, post-midterm
departmental meeting. He was at her house,
they had been drinking. Object: *Direct.* Mood:

*Indicative.* Number: *Many, many times.*
It began in earnest innocence, swaying beneath
the implausible pitch of midnight's infinitive.

But then her genitives began to tingle
and that dangling modifier of his? Well,
it did not dangle for long. Their copula

was quick but smooth like a diphthong.
*Should we have done that?*, she asked. *No?*
*Let's do it again!* And she was euphemism

under his palate, which cracked into halves
like the split in a compound noun. And even before
he ruptured her hyphen, she came

to understand why a man must always,
*always* trill his *r*'s. *Oooh* said she
with an umlaut's latitude, *What a strong verb*

*you are!* And so they conjugated. Elatedly.
And when he *inserted his expletive*,
when he *interjected*, when he

*filled her pause*, she discovered,
surprisingly enough, that "to ejaculate"
did not simply mean shouting *Fire!*

in a crowded lobby, and that syntax
was indeed a grammar well worth its price.
And it was nice how his semantics

spat forth from his diction. *So very nice*
this friction that rasped her insides sore.
No longer would she grope around the metaphor.

For *who're* is just a stroke away from *whore*.
And while life *is* more than sex, it's not much more.

## De Profundis

*He sent darkness and made it dark.*
*Psalm 105:28*

I draw closed like a curtain in your absence.
I torch the sugar, I swill the absinthe,
I renew the old suicide, gladly. A noose of laments

have I trussed to the chapel's top rafter.
Your luminous mysteries loom dim and disastrous.
Come and save me, Master.

Mercy, pity, peace, love.
*Jesus.* What became of us?
When I loosed my hair as the harlot does,

my agonies dragged me hither. I shiver now alone,
a damn, damp woman in a dressing gown,
ill-fit for the dressing-down

your *Going* and your *Gone* betrothed
me. Let the sad self spill her sad, sad story: *It was cold*
*that year, and no one liked the books I wrote.*

*And about my throat, I wore*
*the reprimanding hands of men who swore*
*that they adored me.* But the butcher's

bride is just another slab of flesh he cleaves.
Simpering and thirty-three,
I did not know what you would have of me

but an apology. At thirty-four,
you are the longish thing I long for,
Lord.

And so I whore these corridors of darkness.
I troll the streets like a shamefaced
trollop, your fancy woman anointed in nard, in piss.

I am bliss without your blessing,
a stammering
silence accidentally

spoken. Born again,
but with a birth defect, and broken—
for what the devil claims he rarely abandons.

Out of the depths, have I cried
unto thee, have desired but thee,
have blighted thee with my sleight-of-hand wiles

or at least I have tried to.
Beneath the fright of a lightless moon,
I see it was no use. It is no matter that I ache for you—

and God, *I do*—there's hardly a corpse that's crawled from her crypt.
Let them carve into my gravestone *O Thou Hypocrite.*
Should this praying kill me, I'll have earned it.

# For the Bruxist

My faith in your jaw's aplomb has waned to near eclipse.
Your molars splinter into tiny bits.
The fragments tangle in my hair like goddamned nits,

and I'm crushed into pulp by your palate, scraped
to a brokeheart paste your enamel abrades.
So the landscape of your mouth is reshapen.

*And I hate it.* The bone of your tongue knows nothing.
For the occlusion, I conclude it, jointly, something
misconstrues us. *Thus:* I masticate myself, O Cavity.

No more am I the milk-tooth bride who you de-veiled
two Junes ago. These hazel eyes have glazed, then paled.
I put on my best sleep for you, but *Christ,* I failed.

# Folie à Deux, Ménage à Trois

She is comely. You are charming. I am drunk.
So we teeter on the precipice of this suggestion, the three of us,

our novice incompetence showing like leg through a sheer skirt
until someone musters nerve enough to insert

the odd thumb into the old waistband
and we proceed—*hand in hand in hand*—

into a back, black bedroom where we will swill a little nip
of something gin, and then begin by stripping

out of our usual selves
*(the gin helps).*

She is tiny. You are Herculean.
I am being felt by fingers of indeterminate origin,

for, where one of us ends, another two someones take up.
With six square inches of sex-flesh between us,

and a triad of urgent, urogentital swellings,
there's plenty for show-and-telling.

She is crossroad. You are junction. I am a Christian,
though clearly an inferior one,

for I yawn my sleepy legs as wide apart
as they will open. But the sinning is the better part

of the repentance. And the flesh is so willing and sweet.
We are Trinity. One in Three. Holy,

Holy, Holy *We*. She is delightful.
You are a mouthful. And I am doubtful

we'll be altogether proud in the morning.
But we are all so horny

that the sheets beneath us snag on our protrusions.
Ah, what dead of night wooings

we do beneath the moon. And who we screw
ourselves into.

She is Aphrodite. You are Priapus.
I am Impropriety in one of her kinky disguises.

This does not surprise us as I fondle the sway of her apple-
round breast, as our limbs take to mingling

like party guests, cock in the one hand, tail in another.
We bleed into each other like watercolors

*(and have I mentioned just how soused we are?)*.
She strums you like a harp

wherewith you whistle as a kettle.
Me, I ride you like a bicycle,

legs in the air and whirling.
You have *two* girlies,

a pair of pipe-fitting wenches
happy to wrench

every inch of your plumbing.
She is frenching. You are clenching.

I am coming.

# A Force is a Push or a Pill

*You are my enemy,* I snap
at no one in particular.

And no one in particular
hears me.

Such is my infirmity.
Always in the deep dark,

my heart beats like a beating heart,
*irrationally even,*

even as the black silence of sleep
locks its hot door upon me,

my shoddy, my so-for-nothing
self. In the interminable hour,

I am no riddle. I do not figure out.
But a force is a push or a pill

and desire alone will never tell
the truth.

Like: I would have killed myself for you.
Like: I may already have.

# Post—

*after Simon Armitage's "To His Lost Lover"*
*Now they are no longer*
*any trouble to each other...*

And the letter she deigns to write might begin:
*Well, Dear, I am drunk again.*
Or: *Last night, I dreamt I was Magdalene*

*and you were Jesus Christ.*
Or: *Isn't it nice*
*how we've avoided such backbite*

*betrayals as I'm sure we both once planned*
*to carry out?* And she could expound
upon this, explaining how the Left Hand

knew not what or who the Right Hand did,
knew not that it hid, clenched like a fist
in his pocket, ever an inch

away from waving goodbye. *It wasn't*
*anybody's fault. Our kismets*
*got crossed, or—shall I muse?—the descant*

*of our song trailed off and the melody*
*couldn't survive on its own.* And her script, sloppy
as gin would admit: *Often, I think on you fondly.*

But both will confess that the bed they shared was flawed
by frame, by farewell. How well he said
her name when he meant *Someone Else*, and the hushed,

dim sinning of the linens.
And then,
how it ended.

Still bright in her mind, that sorehead spree
of insult added upon injury.
And, her misery. Nevertheless, her letterhead might read

in twelve point Garamond a fresh nomenclature.
For what he once cut loose, she will have sutured
to another. And really, seeing as they had no future

*(did they?)*, this will sting him, but briefly,
a bee in his boxers, chiefly,
though—*and truly*—her intent is not to maim. Fifty

years from today, neither will quibble
over how or when at last it came to pass, but will instead recall
with flinching precision how subdermal

like a splinter did they burrow underneath each other's skin.
And she, she might remember again, but warmly, the dimple in his chin,
and the thin, tinny rasp in his off-guard voice, the backspin

on his tennis serve. His nerve. Or, what noise he made above her,
coming. Or, the haste by which he abandoned her,
going. And yet, there

have been such interim
moments wherein she thinks she catches sight of him
in street-crowds, where she rushes through the bedlam,

calls his name out to a stranger. In a bar
once, as she lingered over Scotch and licked with her finger
the rim of the glass, she swore

she heard him laughing right behind her. She spun about so quick
she burned her coat on someone's cigarette. It wasn't him, but a fragment
of what could have been anyone guised in the scent

of his cologne and the dumb, blunt drone
of that old Ha-ha. Dare she disclose how many phone
calls she aborted half-way through the dial? The gallstone

ache from where her heart ought be but isn't any more? Or
that hers is become a different heart, a heart of the corkboard
strain? She bobs and floats in a neap tide's wake. *Before,*

*were we so bedriddenly smitten, we did not quit*
*the house for thirteen days.* And After? *Shit*
*if I know.* This, will she write bereftly,

for *Everything gets ruined in the moonlight,*
*especially the moonlight.* And she will sign
in her pie-eyed scribble, a surprisingly

barefaced P.S.: *As pain is to suffering, sex is to lust,*
*and what I should not say is what I must.*
*That I forgot how quickly forgetfulness comes.*

*Also. I forgot to love.*

# Bad Friday

The light went dim, and then demented.
And that was the queasy last of it.

When they finagled his body down from its hanging tree,
they gave it to me

and said *Take, grieve.* I sent the others home
and I arrayed him in his tomb

like a shop girl dressing up a window.
*What a display.* I anointed his brow

with balsam and ointment.
I held him tightly, close as a confidence,

and yet: *It is no secret.* No one knows
what happens when the black hole

of death collapses upon a person's acres.
I clothed him in a sheath of gauze, pale as paper.

I draped his eyes with widow's mites.
I canted the prayers of an Israelite wife.

I set his features. I combed his beard.
And then I disappeared

into the slow, sore torture
that is mourning. And *mourning*

is, by Christ, the very word for it because it *dawns*
on you. A cold stretch of day yawning

open, the inevitable sunrise
of solitude. *Truly this I tell you*: More dire

than the orgy of the golden calf,
is the story of the god who breaks in half.

That was a couple of days ago.
And now,

an unblunted light numbs the white horizon
and a redolence of meadowrue fills the garden

air with evergreen. There are flowers all around me.
*How long have I been sleeping?*

His stone is gone.
This room is empty. I am alone.

Where he went I cannot guess.
And his absence feels worse than his death

did, if that makes any sense.
It is just after six

in the goddamn morning.
I am but a wasteland of worry.

Did someone come and steal him
from the grave? All that remains are the linens

that I left him in, aromatic, sheer
and ghostly. An angel says he is not here.

*Where the fuck is he?*

# Strange Woman

*After Proverbs 7*

She searches the sky for a god who will reach down and love her.
She seeks the arms of a lust that would stretch out to have her.
She shudders like a whore in a rickety chair.
She plaits ribbons of pain in her hair.

She sings unruly songs in strident keys.
Her feet abide in no man's custody.
She is pity's shabby bride, and lechery's courtesan.
Mistress of a never-to-rise-again sun.

She tinctures her wines according to your desires.
In her bed, Hell is always and only fire.
You can set her apart like surfeit, delirious tither.
But no. She won't be faithful to you either.

But hearken: The Goodman is gone and she will flatter you.
Use her. She will let you.

# Whoreheart

I am the bridge you dare not cross.
An ice-floe that won't be defrosted.
A signpost in your dense, damp woods.
The serrated flower of the snakeroot.
A doe amid the beeweed.
And the rocks in the field hurt my feelings.

And I'm the spendthrift wench in debtor's jail.
The wound that won't quite heal.
That little Judas sitting on your shoulder.
The irregular bread of a mendicant's supper.
A disastrous truth told in candor.
I'm the milksap of the oleander.

And mine are the cyanide sockets of almonds.
I'm the kink in the appleworm, the dolmen
that entombs you. I am not safe nor sorry.
Swollen Moses, *am I your darling?* I shall part
like a red and willing sea. *And do I simile?*
Take off your metaphor and face me.

And I am the ocean in which you'll drown.
Abundantly black, I yawn and I drawl.
I'm calm but for aggregate, gathering storms.
And I swarm your bed like a charm
of fiend finches. And last night I rained inches,
and hours. And I am the pitcher

plant's practical talent. The flytrap, the pie plate,
the oblate, the shrew. The mistake you made
too late to undo. The jackscrew to your threaded rod.
*A fraud.* I'm the pussycat of need. Your defeat. Your pall.
And I loom for you like a terrible end.
And I am not your friend.

# Surely Come the Days

Surely come the days
when the heart of the matter at hand
is my heart in your hand,
in desiccated halves.

Surely come the days
when my white dress pales
to a ghoster shade of painful,
and for no discernable

purpose, neither curious
nor clinical. So then come the days
of your callous and cynical mimicry.
When you will say mean things to me

and mean them. When the four a.m.
goring of my corpus informs me
there's a kindness you don't practice,
and never will. So the consequence

of my eagerness is my solitude.
An insufficient answer, but it's true.
And yet, the lips I kiss you with
have never been my own. So wilts

the lily on a vine of morose hours.
Surely as the bergamot sours,
comes the age of recurring oblations.
When my ablutions occur in unstable

waters. When my hells run hotter.
When you take to the hills. When I sort
our photos into stacks of yes and no, no, no.
When each of my hungers runs to the bone

and our account of unpaid devastations
is in arrears. Surely come my tears,
as tears will surely, sorely come.
Surely come the days of numbness.

Days of my despondence, days
of your revenge. Days when you are keen
to kill the fairy-wren you can't quite catch.
And surely come the days when I will hatch

the very plan that might halt you in those tracks.
When I change my name to Dido. And strike a match.

# Riddles

When a door is not a door it is a jar.
And if a market's not a grocery it's... *bizarre.*

If Christ is whining in the cellar, then who becomes the blood?
When I'm irrepressible, I'm very, *very* good.

Either your face is not your face, or I am drunk and mistaken,
For the love we lack in lovemaking, we counterweigh with complication.

What's yours and mine is *hours.* Our minutes contravene.
The heaven in your hands has made you kingly, but obscene.

Eros shot his arrows, now I quiver on your floor.
When a fish is not a fish, it is the Lord.

# Aphrodesia

She of the lovesick,
She of the mandrake,
She of the woodcock,
She of the plover's egg,

She of the lamprey,
She of the marjoram,
She of the countercharm,
She of the doldrum,

She of the aniseed,
She of the philter,
She of the orchids,
Sword-leaved and ladyslipper,

She of the heart-sleeve,
She of the undergloom,
She of the foxglove,
She of the thunderstones,

She of the motherland,
She of the moth,
She of the brothel,
She of the broth,

She of the thumbscrew,
She of the shrieking,
She of the hedge sparrow,
She of the fucking,

She of the snakeroot,
She of the cuttlefish,
She of the passionfruit,
She of the dervish,

She of the loosestrife,
She of the penis,
She of the afterlife:

Venus.

# X Marks the Spot

Of a hard departure.
Of my impending torture.
Of the inclement weather we clothed ourselves in.
X marks the famine that did us in.

X marks the city of my skin-and-bone sinning.
Of the skylark's ascent to her ending.

Of the Lent I spent in penance.
Of that last, lonely sentence I spoke.
The one I'd hoped would scold you into shame.
Of the name I did not take.
Of the name you did not offer.
X marks the place where we disaster-ed.

*You bastard.*

X marks the nest of the blackbird, preening.
X marks me, his dirty wing.
X scars the heart of everything.

Of palms and hosannas.
Of alms laid at your feet.
Of the calm before the come:
My deepest wound, the sweetest one.

Of the soon-ness.
The ruined day, thick of clouds that consumed us.

Of the dress I let drop in your house, the naked I was beneath it.
X marks the stain on your sheet, the deed we completed.
X marks the center of my clinging defeatedness.

Oh simple orifice you made complex!
X marks the site of a sadness that aches me.
Of your face so debatable, I'm never sure I've seen it.
Of my amateur kindness, your professional cruelty.
Of the particular glee we convened against the oak tree.
The one into which you carved our star-signs.
And the dark, starved prayers I enshrined there.
X marks the smooth of your hair.
*As I soothed my fingers through its gloss.*

Of this loss.

Of these hands, which tossed you off.
And these lips, which turned you on.
Of the trick you bluffed wherein I fell in love.

Of the blunt, bad Monday when goodbye was said, and *meant.*
Of a bed.
Of a rust-headed avocet wading in our stagnancy.
Of this tragedy of memory, a rare and vagrant albatross.
Of the vacant stare you betroth me.

*I can't deny your eyes.*

And midnight will always frighten me blind.

X marks the zone where our *yes* became *knowing.*
X marks my breast where your mouth once went roaming.
X marks the *over* I'm *under* going.

X marks our new *nothing.*

# Failed: A Feeble Fable

But there's no moral to this,
No parable despite the kiss,
No tale. *Oh, oh it is a sad thing,*
As we still our chins to stone and suffering,

And winter fastens to our spines
Like drunkenness to wine.
Love, your hands are plain as air,
And in their starkness, stiff, impaired.

But ours is an answer in want of a question,
A lubricant lacking its friction.
A sin sans Christian who'll confess it.
A skirt without a girl to undress from it.

Indeed and very indeed. We *might* have made
Some proper pair of candlesticks displayed
Atop a mantle in a house with lust and laughter.
We won't, of course. There is no ever after.

# Magdalene's Hymn

First it is your face.
But then your face gives way

to facelessness.
Yes, Lord, yes: Open my lips,

and by my mouth
I will proclaim exactly how

our *ah* becomes *alas*. Green
as a peach, easy

to bruise, I am Judas
enough to kiss

you without flinching,
an irrevocable wench

adorned in sackcloth and ash.
I'm trouble in your flesh,

an ice-field of intemperate agonies.
Last night on my knees,

you forgave me these things.
You gave me a ring.

A poisoner's pillbox.
A circlet of hemlock.

An epoch of sleepwalk and rot.
Yours is the cot

I lie upon.
And yours is the cross I will someday die on.

And here, here is the dirge
that will urge

me to that doom:
*I will not do without you.*

That's a fact,
cold and ragged.

Yes, Lord, yes. I am one half of nothing.
Bless this blessing.

Curse me.
There's worse

on my conscience than love.
*God above,*

you are the ache in which I live,
the abdication that I grieve.

The cipher I can't quite read.
*I plead:*

The sky is marred by the darkest of signs.
I beg you not destroy me with your eyes.

# The Thirty-Four Sorrows and a Solitary Anguish of Irreparable Regret

*(One.)*
That this is a poem of sex and death.
And I am *both*.

*(Two.)*
That I gave a little bird to my lover,
But my lover gave it back to me. *See?*

*(Three.)*
When *Midnight, my Coquette,*
Was what he said though never meant.

*(Four.)*
When I catch myself imagining sex with R.
*(I have imagined this before.)*

*(...)*
And how parallel lines will eventually meet.
And how the beauty of hell is its symmetry.

*(...)*
That with a wrench of the knob and a quick,
Crisp click, came the rattle of a latch: *Exactly.*

*(...)*
Does he not remember
That I fed him from my fingers?

*(Eight.)*
How the heart is but a wall of throbbing striations.
Each a devastation.

*(...)*
That mine is a shame-faced story.
*For which. I am. Beyond sorry.*

*(...)*
That a thief on a cross is all I am. That I sleep in a bed
Of satins and sham. That I'm alone, without a man. *Damn.*

*(...)*
And how I dwelt in his ghost chamber's basement.
I remind: That was *my* mouth he moistened.

*(...)*
How my secrets bore into deeper holes
Like shipworms through a wooden hull.

*(Thirteen.)*
Once, there were men with mercies and madness.
They wrung out my skin like wet rags.

*(...)*
*Let us take the train*, I said.
But he went on ahead.

*(Fifteen.)*
And still! I gave myself to be consumed,
Weeping like a wound.

*(...)*
*Worse married than dead* was what I said,
But with a ring, I thee wed. *Instead.*

*(...)*
And it was a black bird, a bad bird.
Infernal bird—*my gravitas.*

*(...)*
That I was the dupe of his déjà vu,
An indivisible zero halved by two.

*(...)*
But I would not let him go until he blessed me.
(Oh Lord—*my Christ!*—undress me!)

*(Twenty.)*
That it ought to be known I was born this way,
With indiscriminate tendencies.

*(...)*
*Weren't I the woman you wanted?*
*Wasn't me?*

*(...)*
All desire will dry to dust.
Likewise: *Us.*

*(Twenty-three.)*
Therefore, having not yet done with grief,
I will mostly opt for the relief a good fuck brings.

*(...)*
Alas, every juice I pour is love.
But no two hands will ever be enough.

*(Twenty-five.)*
Oh how my broken heart betrays me!
Oh how my poems cliché me!

*(...)*
That woman you love? *She doesn't exist.*
She never will. *(She never did.)*

*(...)*
And there is nowhere left to go.
*Oh.*

*(...)*
How ours is a union that begins and ends in pain.
When it is over we do it again.

*(...)*
For, over *all things* is the heart deceitful.
Often mean, hardly meaningful—

*(Thirty.)*
And from the bone meal of my chest will bloom—
*Very soon*—a singular poppy of doom—

*(...)*
And when I catch myself imagining sex with you—
*We do.*

*(...)*
Oh you who I love who I do not love,
My cup would run over except I have no cup—

*But...*

*(Thirty-three.)*
Years—*and years*—will pass
And I will yearn—*and I will yearn*—for you—

*(Thirty-four.)*
There's nothing left to do but cry
Though I've forgotten how to—

*(AND)*
Because I want to sit down next to you,
I do not sit down next to you.

# Nightboat

*after Mark 4:35-41*

We were alone and all was safe,
though the soft, sad suck of the waves

as they lapped the woodbeams of the bow
seemed to warn that something strange or forlorn was about

to pass. It was late, four hours into the deepest dark
at least, and a full watch yet to fear before the spark

of dayrise flared.
I ran my hands through his hair

and I rested my cheek
on his shoulder. I dared not speak,

though heavy on my breast
was an unsaid word, a knot of breath,

a choke vine twined about a tree.
But he was with me. And we

were alone. A gull skimmed
the water like a well-skipped stone and the sealskin

silk of his beard felt nice
against my face.

And then it began to rain. The downpour poured down
beseechingly. So I begged my mouth

from his feet to his knees
to his pleasing

to the muskroot bloom that sprung from the bud of his thighs.
He shut his eyes

against the moon, and a salt wind buffed his lips
as if

stored in the blow of the airstream was a yearning
or an unnamed grief. Or relief. Or maybe, it was nothing.

But inches and hours rained.
And the me of little faith

believed only that the world might perish in my throat.
We rocked the boat.

A cyclone urged.
We swelled like a stormcloud, then burst,

*then burst*. And he, he rested easily
having subsided my seas. And in our sleep,

we dreamed of bridal beds.
*Pilot me*, I prayed. And he did.

# The Nothing That's Left

It is always—*and only*—goodbye.
A haunting, irrevocable *No*,
to which the heavy heart responds: *Don't go.*

I do not blame the trains.
Even the dead are alive to God.
But there are many ways to be dead.

Like when hours ensue into hells.
And we become great riddles to ourselves
and the devils that indwell

us. And so it was: Potent
but petty nights of tragic desires.
*Ours.*

Oh glass eye of foresight!
Oh cataract of afterthought!
I didn't do anything wrong,

I did *everything* wrong.
How susceptible I was to sadness.
To the savor of a first or final kiss.

To the wistful narcissus in bloom.
*To you.* Weeks
pass. I am weak.

The marrow of the matter?
*No matter.* Your soul is saved.
Let not my life be wasted.

Yes. It's always goodbye.
But goodbye is the very least of it.
And *cicatrix*

is just a fancy name for scar.
So I hold out. I tender no notice.
And yet I know this

much: You were the glint in my undergloom,
A body in my archway.
I'll never say

we're through. And so I throb
and thrum and hum and grieve.
And I'll believe and I'll seek

and—god damn it—I will bleed
until there is nothing that's left
but the nothing that's left.

That's something, *isn't it?*

# Notes & Acknowledgements

An earlier draft of "The Ellipses We Consist Of" was published in the inaugural (2004) issue of *The Langdon Review* as "Bed of Sighs."

"Judas Hausfrau," "Crux," "Harlot," "Post—," and "Lament" appeared in the October 9, 2006, issue of *No Tell Motel*.

"The Assignation" and "The Men We Marry, the Men We Fuck" appeared in *The Bedside Guide to No Tell Motel: Second Floor* (No Tell Books, 2007).

"The Clockmaker's Mistress Knows Complications" was published in *The National Poetry Review*. Note: † In horology, a "complication" on a watch or a clock is any feature beyond that of a basic hours, minutes, and seconds movement, such as the date, a chronograph, the display of the moon's phases, etc.

"Sadness is a Tower," "The Heart," "A Force is a Push or a Pill," and "The Thirty-Four Sorrows and a Solitary Anguish of Irreparable Regret" appeared in *MiPOesias*.

"Despair is the Only Unforgivable Sin," and "An Oracle Concerning the Melancholic Concubine" were featured in the online journal *42opus*.

"Aphrodesia" and "Why Hast Thou?" appeared in issue 1.5 of the online journal ~*~WOMB~*~.

The litany of herbs and plants in "Aphrodesia" are purported aphrodisiacs.

"La Linguiste" is dedicated to my linguist friend and former German teacher, Guido Halder.

The next to last line of "Whoreheart" is an adulterated translation of a line from J. S. Bach's Cantata #90: *Es reißet euch ein Schrecklich Ende (A terrible end looms for you).*

The poet wishes to thank the following readers for their assistance with the book in all its stages, and for their cheering on of the poet through all *her* stages: Craig Arnold, Jill Baumgaertner, Bruce Covey, Lyman Grant, Paula Mendoza-Hanna, Neil Ellis Orts, Jessica Piazza, Louisa Spaventa, Susan Stayton, and Laura Van Prooyen.

The poet is grateful for the artwork of Cynthia Large and the design talents of Meghan Punschke.

The poet humbly recognizes the unflagging support with which her very patient and über accommodating husband, Axel, has buttressed her day-to-day life.

Lastly—*hardly leastly!*—the poet desires to make known her sincerest appreciation and most manic of gratitude for the work of the clever, the classy, the exceedingly comely Reb Livingston: My publisher. My friend.

## About the Poet

Jill Alexander Essbaum's published work includes *Heaven*, the winner of the 1999 Bakeless Prize, and *Oh Forbidden*, a cycle of erotic sonnets. A fourth collection, *Necropolis*, is forthcoming from neoNuma Arts (Spring, 2008).  She lives in Switzerland.

Jill can be reached via email at jilly@essbaum.com.

# Also by No Tell Books

## 2008

*Personations*, by Karl Parker

## 2007

*The Bedside Guide to No Tell Motel - 2nd Floor*, editors Reb Livingston & Molly Arden

*Never Cry Woof*, by Shafer Hall

*Shy Green Fields*, by Hugh Behm-Steinberg

*The Myth of the Simple Machines*, by Laurel Snyder

## 2006

*The Bedside Guide to No Tell Motel*, editors Reb Livingston & Molly Arden

*Elapsing Speedway Organism*, by Bruce Covey

*The Attention Lesson*, by PF Potvin

*Navigate, Amelia Earhart's Letters Home,* by Rebecca Loudon

*Wanton Textiles*, by Reb Livingston & Ravi Shankar

**notellbooks.org**